SOUTH AFRICA
the land

Domini Clark

A Bobbie Kalman Book

The Lands, Peoples, and Cultures Series

Crabtree Publishing Company

The Lands, Peoples, and Cultures Series

Created by Bobbie Kalman

Coordinating editor
Ellen Rodger

Project development
First Folio Resource Group, Inc.
  Pauline Beggs
  Tom Dart
  Kathryn Lane
  Debbie Smith

Editing
Tara Steele

Photo research
Robyn Craig

Design
David Vereschagin/Quadrat Communications

Separations and film
Dot 'n Line Image Inc.

Printer
Worzalla Publishing Company

Consultants
Leon Jordan and Claudina Ramosepele, South African High Commission; Dr. Joseph R. Manyoni, Department of Sociology and Anthropology, Carleton University; Tshepoeng Mohohlo, Principal, Uitspandoorns Farm School; Professor T. Sono, Professor Extraordinary, Graduate School of Management, University of Pretoria and President, South African Institute of Race Relations; Michael Titlestad, University of South Africa

Photographs
Tony Angermayer/Photo Researchers: p. 20 (left); Archive Photos: p. 28 (right); Anthony Bannister/ Photo Researchers: p. 8–9 (bottom); Geoff Bryant/ Photo Researchers: title page; Les Bush/Link: p. 21 (bottom); Corbis/Charles O'Rear: p. 3, p. 31 (right); Corbis/Paul Velasco, ABPL: p. 15 (top);
Nigel J. Dennis/Photo Researchers: cover, p. 11 (bottom), p. 18 (bottom), p. 19 (bottom), p. 23 (top right); Chad Ehlers/International Stock Photo: p. 24 (top); Orde Eliason/Link: p. 12 (top), p. 21 (right); Gwynneth Glass/Link: p. 23 (left); Clem Haagner/ Photo Researchers: p. 22 (bottom); M.P. Kahl/Photo Researchers: p. 22 (top); Hubertus Kanus/Photo Researchers: p. 4 (top), p. 7 (top), p. 8 (top), p. 14 (right); G.C. Kelley/Photo Researchers: p. 16 (both), p. 20 (right); Robin Laurance/Photo Researchers: p. 9 (top), p. 10; Jason Lauré: p. 4 (bottom), p. 7 (bottom), p. 12 (bottom), p. 13 (top), p. 24 (bottom), p. 25 (top), p. 26 (right), p. 27 (top), p. 29 (both), p. 30, p. 31 (left); Maratea/ International Stock Photo: p. 28 (left); Material World/Impact: p. 27 (bottom); Richard T. Nowitz: p. 11 (top); M. Timothy O'Keefe/ International Stock Photo: p. 26 (left); Porterfield/ Chickering/Photo Researchers: p. 14 (left), p. 15 (bottom); Carl Purcell: p. 5, p. 19 (top); Reuters/Mike Hutchins/Archive Photos: p. 17 (bottom); South African Tourism: p. 18 (top); K.H. Switak/ Photo Researchers: p. 23 (bottom right); Tropix/ A. Mountain: p. 17 (top); Tropix/Ian Spark: p. 25 (bottom); Ingrid Mårn Wood: p. 13 (bottom), p. 21 (top left)

Map
Jim Chernishenko

Illustrations
Marie Lafrance: icon
David Wysotski, Allure Illustrations: back cover

Cover: Gemsboks graze on tufts of grass in Kalahari Gemsbok National Park.

Title page: *Leucospermum cuneiforme* is a flower native to Cape Province.

Icon: A baobab tree appears at the top of each section.

Back cover: The springbok is South Africa's national symbol.

Published by
Crabtree Publishing Company

PMB 16A 350 Fifth Ave.	360 York Road, RR 4,	73 Lime Walk
Suite 3308	Niagara-on-the-Lake,	Headington
New York	Ontario, Canada	Oxford OX3 7AD
N.Y. 10118	L0S 1J0	United Kingdom

Cataloguing in Publication Data
Clark, Domini, 1979-
    South Africa, the land / Domini Clark.
        p.cm. -- (The lands, peoples, and cultures series)
    "A Bobbie Kalman book."
    Summary: Explores the beauty of South Africa, from Table Mountain near Cape Town to the dry veldt in the north.
    ISBN 0-86505-315-4 (paper) -- ISBN 0-86505-235-2 (RLB)
    1. South Africa--Description and travel--Juvenile literature.
    [1. South Africa--Description and travel.] I. Title.II.Series.
DT1738.C58 2000
968--dc21   LC 99-042506

Contents

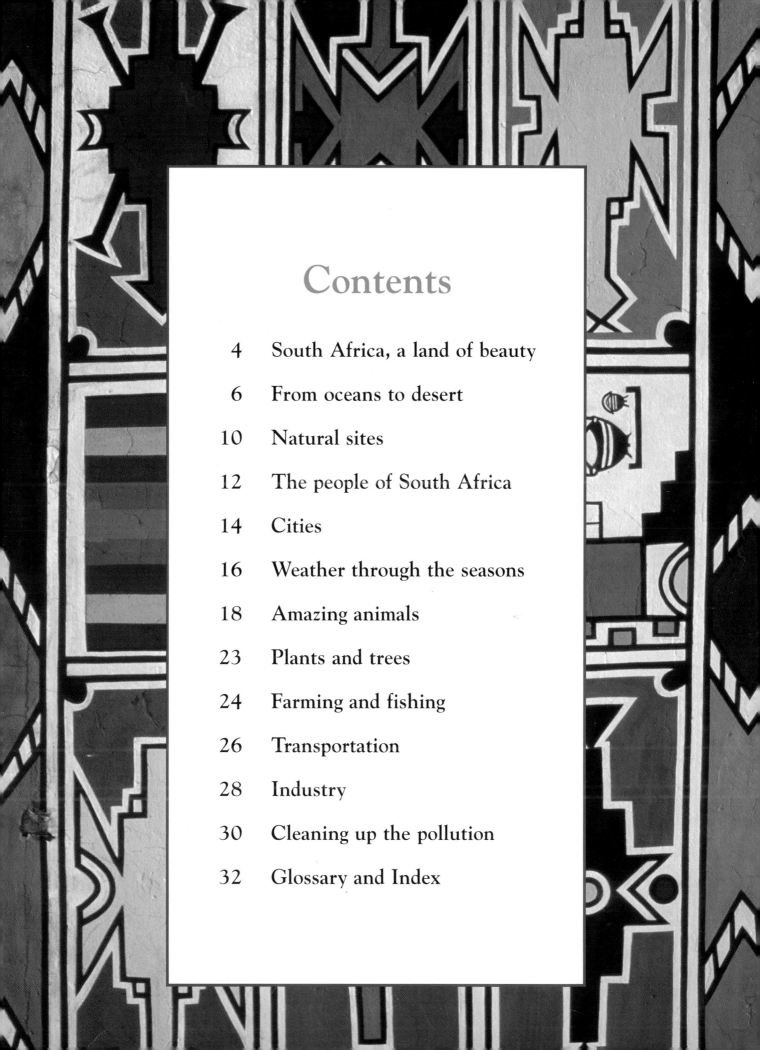

4   South Africa, a land of beauty

6   From oceans to desert

10 Natural sites

12 The people of South Africa

14 Cities

16 Weather through the seasons

18 Amazing animals

23 Plants and trees

24 Farming and fishing

26 Transportation

28 Industry

30 Cleaning up the pollution

32 Glossary and Index

South Africa, a land of beauty

(top) A village is nestled among lush, rolling hills.

(right) Whirlpools in the Blyde River wore away rock to create cylindrical shapes.

According to legend, a woman named Mujaji once ruled a vast **empire** in central Africa. Mujaji, who was also known as the Rain Queen, had the power to make it rain if she was pleased or dry up the land if she was angry. Many years ago, the Rain Queen led her people south to escape an invasion of grasshopper-like locusts. The people traveled for many years until they came to a vast, dry plain with a great mountain range rising beyond it. When Mujaji saw this desolate place, she knew it would be home to her people. She walked to the top of a lone hill and made it rain night after night until the valleys and plains were green with new life. The extraordinary place to which she brought rain was the land of South Africa.

(opposite) South Africa's dramatic shoreline plunges into the Indian Ocean along the southern coast.

From oceans to desert

South Africa lies at the southern tip of the African continent. Water surrounds the country on three sides, but there are few rivers and streams inland. Some rivers have no water at all during the dry season. Even the western part of the Orange River, South Africa's longest river, is almost completely dry for most of the year. The east part is a source of **hydroelectric power** and water for crops.

Lesotho and Swaziland

South Africa is divided into nine provinces: Western Cape, Eastern Cape, KwaZulu-Natal, Northern Cape, Free State, North-West, Gauteng, Mpumalanga, and Northern Province. If you look at a map, however, you might think there were two more provinces: Lesotho and Swaziland. South Africa completely surrounds the country of Lesotho and it borders the country of Swaziland on three sides.

SOUTH AFRICA

N

| 0 | 100 | 200 | 300 km |
| 0 | 100 | 200 | 300 mi |

ZIMBABWE

BOTSWANA

Kruger National Park

MOZAMBIQUE

Northern Province

• Moria

Kalahari Desert

Witwatersrand

Kalahari Gemsbok National Park

NAMIBIA

North West

Pretoria

Johannesburg •

Soweto •

Gauteng

Mpumalanga

SWAZILAND

Drakensberg Mountains

Augrabies Falls

Kimberley •

Free State

KwaZulu-Natal

Bloemfontein •

LESOTHO

Namaqualand

Orange River

• Durban

Northern Cape

GREAT KAROO

Eastern Cape

ATLANTIC OCEAN

Grahamstown •

• East London

Western Cape

Cango Caves •

Oudtshoorn •

Cape Town •

Port Elizabeth •

Cape of Good Hope

INDIAN OCEAN

Coastal plain and interior plateau

White sand beaches and jagged sandstone cliffs stretch along South Africa's coasts. On the beaches, hills of sand, called **dunes**, are shaped by wind. Some dunes are small, but others can be taller than an adult.

In from the coast is a high, flat **plateau** that covers much of the country. Most of the plateau is grassland, which is called the **veld**, but in some parts thorny trees and small shrubs grow.

(right) A ridge of mountains looms beyond the houses and beaches of Cape Town.

(below) Crops grow on the vast plains of the veld.

The sheer cliff faces, called **krantzes,** *and ravines, called* **kloofs,** *make the Drakensberg Mountains a challenging place to hike.*

The Great Escarpment

A long ridge of mountains, called the Great Escarpment, forms a rocky wall that separates the eastern coast from the interior plateau. Water flowing from the mountain peaks rushes through gorges and canyons, and waterfalls pour over cliffs. The most famous part of the **escarpment** is a group of mountains called the Drakensberg, or Dragon, Mountains. Dutch people who settled in this area long ago gave the mountains this name because they thought the line of peaks looked like the scaly ridge along a dragon's spine. People hike, climb, and ride horses in the mountains for days at a time.

(above) The Great Escarpment rises beyond farmers' fields in the province of KwaZulu-Natal.

(left) From the sky, the sweeping dunes of the Kalahari Desert look like an ocean of orange waves.

The Kalahari Desert

The Kalahari Desert lies in the north western part of South Africa and in the neighboring countries of Botswana and Namibia. It rains so rarely in the Kalahari that the riverbeds fill with water only about once every 50 years. Short trees offer a bit of shade to the people and animals living here. Special holes drilled in the earth near riverbeds help the Kalahari's inhabitants reach water that they can drink.

 # Natural sites

South Africa's landforms are truly amazing. Mountains with steep cliffs and flat tops rise above deep gorges, waterfalls carve elaborate caves and tunnels through rocks, and areas of flat land stretch farther than the eye can see.

Table Mountain

Table Mountain overlooks the city of Cape Town. This mountain got its name because it has a flat, squared-off top instead of a peak. Over thousands of years, wind and water **eroded**, or wore away, some of Table Mountain's layers of sandstone, giving it a distinctive shape. If you ride the cable car to the top, you can see all of Cape Town spread out below.

(top) Thick white clouds shroud Table Mountain near Cape Town. This cloud formation is called the "Tablecloth."

The Great Karoo

Millions of years ago, the Great Karoo was a huge swamp where dinosaurs roamed. Today, it is part of the interior plateau and covers one third of South Africa. The Great Karoo gets its name from the Khoikhoi language, and means "land of thirst." Only short, tough grasses and shrubs grow in this area that has so little water.

Koppies

Most of the Great Karoo is flat, but to the south and west are mountain ranges. *Koppies*, which are small, flat-topped hills of ancient volcanic rock covered with grass, also rise out of the land. These hills and mountains appear to change color depending on the time of day, the weather, and how close you are to them. From far away, they look black or dark blue. Up close, they are deep red, yellow, and orange.

The Cango Caves

In the Khoikhoi language, *cango* means "a wet place." Water drips into the Cango Caves from the ground above. The minerals in the water form huge rock columns called **stalactites** and **stalagmites**. Stalactites hang down from the ceilings of the caves, and stalagmites rise in pillars from the ground. Some stalactites and stalagmites grow so large that they connect and form shapes that look like animals, canopy beds, and pipe organs.

(right) Stalactites and stalagmites create an eerie feeling in the Cango Caves.

(below) In the Great Karoo, a **koppie** *appears orange in the light of the setting sun.*

Many people have come to live in South Africa since the first people, the San and the Khoikhoi, settled there about twenty thousand years ago. The San were **nomadic**, meaning they continually traveled, looking for food and shelter. The Khoikhoi hunted animals and gathered wild plants for their food like the San, but they raised sheep and cattle as well. They usually stayed in one place for longer than the San did. Although many San and Khoikhoi married people from other groups, some direct **descendants** of each group still live in South Africa today.

Bantu speakers

A number of peoples migrated to South Africa from more northern parts of the continent, looking for better grazing and farming land. These people spoke the African Bantu languages. Many of today's black South Africans, who make up 75 percent of South Africa's population, trace their roots back to the Bantu speakers. These include the Zulu, Sotho, and Xhosa people.

A San boy squints as smoke from a campfire fills his eyes.

A father stands proudly with his son.

The first European settlers

In the 1400s, people from Europe began sailing to India to establish spice trading routes. On their way, they stopped at the Cape of Good Hope, at the southern tip of South Africa, for supplies. In 1652, a group of Dutch people settled in the area. They set up farms, providing food and supplies to sailors traveling from Holland to India.

As more sailors used the base, more people were needed to work. The Dutch brought slaves from Southeast Asia to work for them. Over time, French and German people joined the Dutch. These people became known as Afrikaners. Together, they developed their own language, traditions, and government.

The arrival of the British

In the late 1700s and early 1800s, the British arrived in South Africa. They first came to Cape Town to prevent France, which was at war with Holland, from invading South Africa. Then, they came to make sure that British sailors on their way to India had a place to restock supplies. Some British people opened businesses in cities such as Cape Town and East London. Others set up sugar **plantations** near Durban and brought people from India to work on their farms. Eventually, the British took control of South Africa and ruled the land.

Separating the people

For many years, all non-white people were treated very poorly in South Africa. In 1948, the government established the system of **apartheid**, which formally **discriminated** against groups of people based on their skin color. The darker the people were, the fewer rights they had. For example, black people could not live in the same neighborhoods or have the same educational and job opportunities as white people.

Girls share refreshments and have a good laugh during a day's outing.

This brother and sister speak Afrikaans, the language of the Afrikaners.

The end of apartheid

Years of protest and violence followed the introduction of apartheid as people fought for their rights and freedoms. Finally, in 1992, the government **abolished** apartheid. In 1994, the first fully **democratic** government was elected to represent all the people of the country. Some South Africans now call their country the "rainbow nation" as a way of recognizing the many people of different skin colors and cultures who live there.

Cities

Over half of South Africa's 41 million people live in cities. Each city has its own character and its own special places to visit.

Cape Town

Cape Town, South Africa's oldest city, is a blend of history and modern life. There are gardens that date back to the time of the Dutch settlers and modern office buildings that line wide busy streets. One of the most popular parts of Cape Town is the Victoria and Albert Waterfront. This waterfront is both a working harbor and a fun place to shop and meet friends.

(above) Johannesburg is a busy, modern city with many office buildings.

(right) At Greenmarket Square in Cape Town, shoppers look for deals at the daily flea market.

14

Soweto

During apartheid, black people were forced to move out of cities and live in areas set up for them on the outskirts. These areas are called **townships**. Soweto, which stands for the **So**uth**we**stern **To**wnships, is just outside of Johannesburg. Many parts of Soweto are very crowded. It is not unusual for several families to live in one small house, or for a yard to be full of one-room homes where married family members live. Other people live in areas called **shantytowns**, which are filled with shacks built of any available material: metal, paper, wood, or cardboard.

When apartheid ended, the government promised to build one million new houses. They also introduced a plan where, for a monthly fee, people could get a piece of land, electricity, and a water tap. On this land, people could build their own home. Even with these plans, however, many South Africans still do not have a place to live.

Johannesburg

Johannesburg was once just a grassy plain. Then, 150 years ago, gold was discovered nearby. Thousands of people came to the area, hoping to strike it rich. Today, Johannesburg is the country's largest city and business center. Huge skyscrapers tower over the traffic-jammed streets. The whole city seems to be in a hurry. People do not even have time to say Johannesburg's entire name; they just call it Jo'burg.

Renaming places

Today, signs of apartheid are being erased from South African towns and cities. Streets, buildings, and dams that were named after pro-apartheid leaders are being renamed with words from African languages. For example, the Hendrik Verwoerd Dam, on the Orange River, was named after a founder of apartheid. It is now called the Gariep Dam. The word Gariep is the San word for "Great River."

Durban is a seaside city where many South Africans of Indian origin live.

Weather through the seasons

South Africa is south of the **equator**. Its seasons are opposite to the seasons north of the equator, in countries such as the United States and Canada. In South Africa, spring and summer last from October to March. Fall and winter last from April to September.

In the west
Most of South Africa is sunny and warm almost all year long. The west coast is usually cooler than the rest of the country because of a **current** of cold water, called the Benguela Current, that flows north from the Antarctic. The west also tends to be drier than other parts of the country, except in the Cape where it rains during the winter.

(below) During a normal year, Kruger National Park has small lakes where animals can refresh themselves.

In the east
The weather in the eastern part of the country is warmer than in the west because of the Agulhas Current. This current flows south from the Indian Ocean, warming the land. Winds from the ocean carry rain inland, especially during the summer. The water quickly evaporates, though, because it is so hot. Winters in the east are dry and warm, although the further north you travel, the more humid it gets. KwaZulu-Natal can be hot and humid with occasional storms that cause huge waves to crash along the shore.

On higher ground

The higher up you are, the cooler the weather is. In South Africa, the interior plateau is higher than other parts of the country, so temperatures are cooler than in surrounding areas. Frost often appears on clear, cold nights and the highest mountain tops are covered with snow year-round.

Drought

About once every seven years, South Africa has a drought. With no rain for months, the soil hardens and cracks until the land looks like it is divided into thousands of puzzle pieces. Riverbeds dry up completely. Plants and animals that depend on the water in the rivers die. To make sure that no water is wasted during a drought, the government limits the amount of water that people can use.

Floods

Sometimes, South Africa gets more rain than it needs. Large amounts of rain fall quickly and suddenly, causing flash floods across the country. Riverbeds overflow and water rushes over the land. More rain can fall during a flash flood than South Africa usually gets in a year!

(left) A student checks a rain gauge to see how much rain has fallen.

Friends play in the surf on a hot New Year's Eve day.

Amazing animals

South Africa is home to many of the most fascinating animals in the world. Of the world's 80 **species** of sea mammals, 39 are found around South Africa, including the porpoise and southern right whale. In this one country, you can see the world's largest land animal, the elephant, and the smallest, the pygmy shrew. Look up and you might see the world's tallest animal, the giraffe. Then, listen closely for the rustling of grass, and try to spot the cheetah, the world's fastest animal, running by. Most of these animals live in **game reserves**, where they are protected from hunters.

African elephants

There are two kinds of elephants: the African elephant and the Indian (or Asian) elephant. African elephants live in South Africa's grasslands and forests. They are larger than Indian elephants and they have bigger ears. Both the male and female African elephants have long tusks, which can weigh as much as 50 kilograms (110 pounds) each!

African elephants travel in herds of 10 to 50. A herd eats so much food that it must keep moving to find more. It is easy to track where elephants have been. Their huge legs crush plants growing where they walk. Their powerful trunks rip leaves off trees and sometimes even tear entire trees out of the ground.

You might be surprised to see penguins in South Africa, but they are found on the west coast, where the cold Antarctic Ocean currents flow.

18

(opposite page) When an elephant feels threatened, it tries to appear even bigger by holding out its huge ears.

Seals bask in the sun on the rocky shores near Cape Town.

A lion watches over his pride in Kruger National Park.

Lions

Lions live in groups called prides. Each pride is made up of lions, lionesses, and cubs. You can easily tell which are the males: they are the ones with the manes around their faces.

Lionesses do most of the hunting. They go out on their own or in small groups, looking for animals such as zebras, antelopes, or even giraffes. Slowly and quietly, they sneak up on their prey. Then, when the lionesses get very close, they sprint after what they hope will be their next meal. Lionesses must work very quickly, since they can run very fast for short distances only. If their chase takes too long, their prey will get away.

Impalas

Impalas, which look like deer, are one of the most common animals in South Africa. They are known for jumping very high and as far as 9 meters (30 feet) at a time. This helps them get away from hungry lions and cheetahs that are hunting them.

Snakes

Two of the world's most dangerous snakes live in South Africa. Pythons slither through tall grasses and attack their victims without warning. They wrap themselves around their prey, crush it to death, and swallow it whole. Pythons are able to swallow remarkably large animals because their jaws are not firmly attached to their skulls.

The black mamba is the fastest known snake. It is twice as long as an average man is tall. This snake kills its prey by biting it. Poison, or **venom**, is injected into its target through its hollow fangs. A mamba's poison could easily kill a human.

(above) A male impala, or buck, with elegant ridged horns takes a cool drink from a water hole.

(left) Mambas grow to 2.5 meters (8 feet) and can use two-thirds of their body length to strike at prey.

A pair of banded mongooses peak out of their burrow. Mongooses can pounce with lightning speed and are skilled snake hunters.

Birds

Over 900 kinds of birds live in South Africa. Hawks, eagles, vultures, and falcons fly over the land. Long-legged pink flamingos wade in shallow lagoons. The kori bustard, the world's heaviest flying bird, makes its home on the grassy plains. Cattle egrets follow herds of cows or rhinos, looking for insects in the dirt that the animals kick up.

(above) Colonies of weaver birds live together in huge nests made of woven grass.

(left) So many ganets flocked to this beach that it is very tricky to find a place to land!

21

Protecting South Africa's animals

About 100 years ago, many of South Africa's animals were in danger of disappearing. People built cities and towns where animals roamed and cut down forests where they lived. Some animals almost became **extinct** because so many people hunted them. Elephants were hunted for their ivory tusks, which were made into carvings and jewelry. Big cats, such as lions and cheetahs, were killed for their hides. To protect these animals, the South African government made it illegal to kill them. It also provided the animals with safe places to live in game reserves.

Kruger National Park

Today, there are game reserves all over the country. The largest is Kruger National Park, which is the size of a small country. Visiting the game reserve is not like visiting a zoo. Here, the animals roam free while people stay in their cars or in special **safari** buses. If they are lucky, they will see some of the more than 140 species of mammals, 110 species of reptiles, 450 species of birds, and 50 species of fish that live here. They can even stay overnight, sleeping in tents or lodges in special areas away from the animals.

(left) A giraffe seems not to notice the birds who are snacking on insects in its fur.

(below) A herd of springbok stand alert in Kalahari Gemsbok National Park.

Plants and trees

In South Africa, you can see grasses, trees, and plants that grow nowhere else in the world. There are trees that look like they are upside down, and grasses that look like silver feathers. There is even an entire kingdom of plants, called the *fynbos*, which grows in the area between Cape Town and Grahamstown. Imagine the world's entire supply of one type of flower living in such a small area!

Floral life in Namaqualand

Every year after the spring rainfall, an incredible explosion of flowers covers the mountains and plains in Namaqualand. Wild daisies, gladioli, mums, irises, freesias, and violets bloom in this normally dry area. Most of these flowers only open when there is bright sunshine, and they do not last for long. They soon shrivel in the hot winds that blow through the area.

South Africa's national flower is the protea. Its spiky bloom can grow as wide as 30 centimeters (1 foot).

Baobab trees

People call the baobab the upside-down tree because of its unusual shape. The tree's branches look like roots and the trunk can be as wide as a car. This shape helps the tree survive. The baobab grows in very dry areas in the most northern part of the country. It stores the little rain it gets in its many branches. When the rivers dry up, elephants break off the branches and drink the water inside them. In the spring, the baobab blooms with large, waxy, white flowers. In the fall, it has furry, egg-shaped fruit.

(above) The meadows of Namaqualand burst with the color fuchsia.

(right) A baobab tree can live for over a thousand years.

Farming and fishing

South Africa's warm temperatures make it perfect for growing a variety of crops. The best area for farming is along the Orange River. There are also huge farms along the coasts, where fruit such as bananas, oranges, mangoes, and apples grow. The fruit is sold at markets around the world.

Grapes

All around Cape Town and along the southern coast of South Africa are large **vineyards**, planted hundreds of years ago by European settlers. Some of the grapes from these vineyards are sold fresh, while others are dried and sold as raisins. Grapes are also crushed and their juice is made into wine. The most famous wine areas are Constantia, just south of Table Mountain, and Stellenbosch and Paarl, east of Cape Town. South African wine is **exported** all over the world and has won awards at international competitions.

At a Stellenbosch vineyard, workers pick grapes by hand.

South Africa has more than 26 million sheep. They were brought to the country 350 years ago by Europeans.

Ranching

The tough ground and short grasses in most parts of South Africa are perfect for raising **livestock**. Cows are raised for milk and meat. Sheep and angora goats are raised mainly for their wool. Most of the livestock are special breeds that have **adapted** to the hot and dry weather in South Africa's grazing areas.

Ostriches

Though ostriches still run wild in South Africa, there were many more in the 1800s. Over a century ago, it became fashionable for women to wear hats decorated with huge ostrich feathers and long scarves of ostrich feathers called boas. So many wild ostriches were hunted and killed in South Africa that they almost became extinct. Farmers started raising the birds and became very rich selling the feathers. These farmers were called feather barons.

Today, very few people wear feathers. Instead, ostriches are raised for their skin, which is made into leather, and for their meat. The town of Oudtshoorn calls itself the Ostrich Capital of the World. Here, visitors can eat an ostrich steak, watch ostrich races, or ride an ostrich. Children can even stand on the huge ostrich eggs. They are so strong that they do not break!

Fishing

The waters around South Africa are some of the best places to fish in the world. Anchovies, herring, sole, mackerel, and lobster are the main catches. The fishing is so good that boats come from all around the world. Unfortunately, some types of fish are caught too often, and they are in danger of disappearing. To prevent this, the government limits the number of fish that a boat can catch.

Fishermen haul in their nets. They have accidentally caught a seal, which they are trying to free.

Three-week-old ostrich chicks gather around to be fed.

Transportation

In the past, South Africans traveled by wagons, buggies, and foot. Their journeys were long and difficult. When the first railway was built in 1860, it became easier to travel around the country. Today, people drive cars, take buses and taxis, and ride bicycles to get from place to place.

Roads

Many roads in South Africa are old routes that early settlers made as they explored the country. Only city roads and highways connecting cities and towns are paved. The rest of the roads are dirt. These roads can be dangerous because they are not always well maintained. Drivers also have to be on the lookout for herds of sheep and cattle that wander onto the roads and block traffic.

Minibus taxis

One way to get around cities, or to get from one city to another, is by minibus taxi. A minibus is supposed to hold twelve people, but it is usually crowded with more. To make matters worse, people's bags are also crammed inside since there is no trunk. For the passengers in the front seat, the ride is not a relaxing one. The passenger beside the driver collects everyone's fare and makes change, while the passenger sitting next to the door has to get out each time the minibus stops to let passengers on and off.

(above) Rain water flows down the ruts of a dirt road.

(right) A minibus loads up with new passengers. Hopefully, everyone else will be able to get on the next bus.

A steam engine speeds along the rails, spewing smoke and carrying a load of coal. South Africa is one of the few countries in the world that still has steam trains.

Trains

Some people travel by commuter, or passenger, trains that run between cities. There are also luxury trains for vacationers. The Blue Train is like a hotel on rails. It has been running since 1946, mainly between Pretoria and Cape Town. The train looks like a giant blue snake as it winds its way around curvy mountain passes. Guests stay in private rooms and even get their own butler! In the front of the train is a special camera that records the scenery. Passengers can watch this view live on television, and feel what it is like to "drive" the train.

A commuter train pulls out of a Soweto train station, taking people to work in Johannesburg.

South Africa has many different industries. Cars, clothes, appliances, and foods such as sugar and flour are made in factories and sold to other countries. Coal is burned in power plants and is used to make steel. Tourists from all over the world vacation here, exploring the beautiful scenery. The industry that South Africa is best known for, however, is mining. There are mines for iron ore, copper, platinum, diamonds, and gold.

Diamonds

According to one story, in 1867, a young boy named Erasmus Jacob picked up a strange pebble from the banks of the Orange River. The pebble turned out to be a diamond. When people heard of the discovery, they came from all over to make their fortune. Each miner worked at a small area, called a **claim**, using a pick and shovel. At first, it was not difficult to mine the diamonds because they were close to the surface. As the diamonds became more difficult to reach, some enterprising people set up a **pulley** system. This system lifted the gravel out of the pits so that miners could reach the diamonds deep down. These people made fortunes and bought up other people's claims.

A worker carefully sorts diamonds at the De Beers Diamond Mines during the late 1800s.

De Beers

By the end of South Africa's diamond rush, two companies owned most of the diamonds. They were the Kimberley Central Mining Company and the De Beers Mining Company. The two companies joined together and became De Beers Consolidated Mines Limited. Today, De Beers is a huge international company that still controls much of the world's diamond production.

Many of the world's largest diamonds were found at the Big Hole in Kimberley. By 1914, the Big Hole was no longer being mined. The huge hole is still there though. It is the largest hole in the world dug by people, rather than machinery.

Gold

In 1886, people digging on a farm discovered huge amounts of gold. This gold was part of a 500-kilometer (300-mile) arc of gold fields stretching across a rocky region in the north called Witwatersrand, or the Rand. Gold is still mined in the area today. The gold is in a part of the rock called the **reef**. Extracting the gold from the reef is very difficult work, partly because South Africa's gold mines are so deep. They are almost 1 kilometer (3000 feet) below ground!

(right) Molten platinum, a valuable precious metal, is poured during the refining process. South Africa is one of the largest platinum producers in the world.

(below) Gold miners drill into the walls of a shaft.

Miners

In the early days, many of the mines' black workers were treated very poorly. They were paid extremely little and were forced to wear shackles around their ankles so they could not escape. Thousands died in accidents when mines collapsed or flooded. Today, many South Africans and people from neighboring countries still work in the mines. Some work for six months to a year before returning home for a few months. Others move to the mines with their families and live in camps built by the mining companies.

Cleaning up the pollution

South Africa's industries have brought money into the country and given people jobs. Unfortunately, they have also damaged the environment and harmed people. Today, government, industry, and environmental groups are working together to stop the pollution caused by these industries and to preserve the spectacular scenery and wildlife of their country.

A hiker enjoys a spectacular view of Blyde River Canyon.

Clean water for everyone

South Africans do not have enough water, and much of the water they do receive evaporates in the hot temperatures or is polluted by chemicals from mining and other industries. The government has built several large dams on the Orange River to store water. Tunnels and canals carry the water to areas where it is needed. The government is also trying to prevent water pollution. New treatments are being used to clean water, and mines and companies that pollute are fined.

Pollution from coal

Coal is South Africa's main source of energy, but burning coal causes pollution. Harmful gases released into the air combine with other gases to form acid. This acid falls to the earth as acid rain. Fish that swim in lakes and rivers polluted by acid rain die. People and animals that drink the water also suffer. Just breathing in gases from coal is dangerous. South Africa has begun to explore sources of energy that are less harmful. **Solar energy**, or energy from the sun's rays, is being used more and more. So is wind power, especially along the coasts where windmills are becoming a common sight.

South Africa tomorrow

South Africa is a land that is as diverse as the people who live there. Deserts, mountains, oceans, and waterfalls are home to spectacular wildlife that live nowhere else on the planet. The people of South Africa are beginning to live in greater harmony with each other and with their environment. They are working to preserve the remarkable land in which they live so that it can be enjoyed by future generations.

School children stage a protest against developers planning to build near Table Mountain.

Windmills are a source of energy in the Kalahari Desert.

31

Glossary

abolish To cancel or put an end to

adapt To adjust or change to fit new conditions

apartheid A policy of separating people based on their race

claim A piece of land identified by miners as their own

current The flow of water along a certain path in the ocean

democratic Elected by the people

descendant A person who can trace his or her family roots to a certain family or group

discriminate To treat unfairly because of race, religion, gender, or other factors

drought A long period of time when no rain falls

dune A mound of sand formed by wind

empire A group of countries under one ruler or government

equator An imaginary line around the middle of the earth that divides the planet into the Northern and Southern Hemispheres

erode To wear away gradually, as with wind and rain wearing away mountain peaks

escarpment A steep hill or long cliff, either at the edge of a plateau or separating land that is at different heights

export To sell goods to another country

extinct No longer in existence, as with dinosaurs

game reserve A park where wildlife is protected from hunters and observed by scientists and tourists

hydroelectric power Electricity produced by the flow of water

livestock Farm animals

nomadic Having no fixed home and moving from place to place in search of food and shelter

plantation A large farm on which crops such as cotton and sugar grow

plateau An area of flat land that is higher than the surrounding land

pulley A simple machine used to lift or lower a heavy load. The load is attached to one end of a rope that runs through a wheel. The load is raised or lowered by pulling or releasing the other end of the rope.

reef A deposit of minerals or ore found in the crack of a rock or between layers of rock

safari A journey or expedition, often to observe wildlife

shantytown A poor area of a city in which most people live in run-down homes or shacks

solar energy Electricity generated from sunlight

species A group of animals or plants that are considered to be of the same type because they share certain characteristics

stalactite A mineral deposit that hangs from the roof of a cave

stalagmite A mineral deposit that points up from the floor of a cave

township An urban area in South Africa in which black people were forced to live

veld An open area of grassland with few trees

venom A poison produced by some snakes, spiders, and other creatures that is passed on to prey by a bite or sting

vineyard An orchard where grapes are grown to make wine

 # Index

acid rain 31
apartheid 13, 15
baobab tree 23
beaches 7
Big Hole 28
birds 21
Blue Train 27
Cango Caves 11
Cape of Good Hope 12
Cape Town 7, 10, 13, 14
cattle egrets 21
coal 28, 31
coastal plain 7
De Beers 28
diamonds 28, 29
Drakensberg Mountains 8
drought 17

Durban 15
elephants 18, 19, 22
floods 17
fynbos 23
game reserves 18, 22
giraffes 18, 19, 22
gold 29
grapes 24
Great Escarpment 8, 9
Great Karoo 10, 11
history 12–13
impalas 20
interior plateau 7, 10
Johannesburg 14, 15
Kalahari Desert 9
Kimberley 28
koppies 10, 11
kori bustard 21

Kruger National Park 22
Lesotho 6
lions 19, 22
mambas 20
map 6
miners 29
minibus taxis 26
mining 28–29
mongooses 21
Namaqualand 23
ocean currents 16, 18
Orange River 6, 30
ostriches 25, 29
Oudtshoorn 25
penguins 18
platinum 29
protea 23
protecting animals 22

provinces 6
pythons 20
ranching 25
renaming places 15
roads 26
seals 19
snakes 20
solar energy 31
Soweto 15
Swaziland 6
Table Mountain 10, 31
townships 15
trains 27
veld 7
water pollution 30
weaver birds 21
wine 24
Witwatersrand 29

1 2 3 4 5 6 7 8 9 0 Printed in the USA 5 4 3 2 1 0 9